ON THE LAUNCH PAD

A Counting Book About Rockets

Thanks to our advisers for their expertise, research, and advice:

Stuart Farm, M.A.
Mathematics Lecturer
University of North Dakota
Grand Forks, North Dakota

Susan Kesselring, M.A.
Literacy Educator
Rosemount-Apple Valley-Eagan
(Minnesota) School District

by **Michael Dahl**

illustrated by **Derrick Alderman**
and **Denise Shea**

The editor would like to thank Kathy Hagood, formerly of the Kennedy Space Center, for her expert advice in preparing this book.

Managing Editor: Bob Temple
Creative Director: Terri Foley
Editor: Brenda Haugen
Editorial Adviser: Andrea Cascardi
Copy Editor: Sue Gregson
Designer: Nathan Gassman
Page production: Picture Window Books
The illustrations in this book were created digitally.

Picture Window Books
A Capstone Imprint
151 Good Counsel Drive
P.O. Box 669
Mankato, MN 56002-0669
1-877-845-8392
www.capstonepub.com

Library of Congress Cataloging-in-Publication Data
Dahl, Michael.
On the launch pad : a counting book about rockets / written by Michael Dahl; illustrated by Derrick Alderman and Denise Shea.

p. cm. — (Know your numbers)
Summary: A countdown from twelve to one as a space shuttle awaits liftoff. Includes bibliographical references and index.
ISBN-13: 978-1-4048-0581-1 (hardcover)
ISBN-10: 1-4048-0581-8 (hardcover)
ISBN-13: 978-1-4048-1119-5 (paperback)
ISBN-10: 1-4048-1119-2 (paperback)

1. Launch vehicles (Astronautics)—Juvenile literature. 2. Rocketry—Juvenile literature. 3. Counting—Juvenile literature. [1.Space shuttles. 2. Rocketry. 3. Rockets (Aeronautics) 4. Counting.] I. Alderman, Derrick, and Shea, Denise, ill. II. Title.
TL785.8.L3 D34 2004

513.2'11—dc22   2003021039

Printed in the United States   4622

TWELVE stars twinkle in the morning sky.

twelve
12

3

ELEVEN workers take care of tasks.

eleven
11

5

TEN engineers watch their screens.

ten
10

7

NINE spotlights shine up on the rocket.

nine
9

9

EIGHT trucks carry the fuel.

SEVEN radar dishes silently stand.

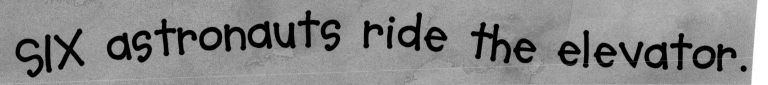

SIX astronauts ride the elevator.

six
6
• • •
• • •

13

FIVE control panels glow and hum.

FOUR windows gleam in the dawn.

THREE launch towers slide away.

18

three
3
••••

19

TWO rocket engines rumble and roar.

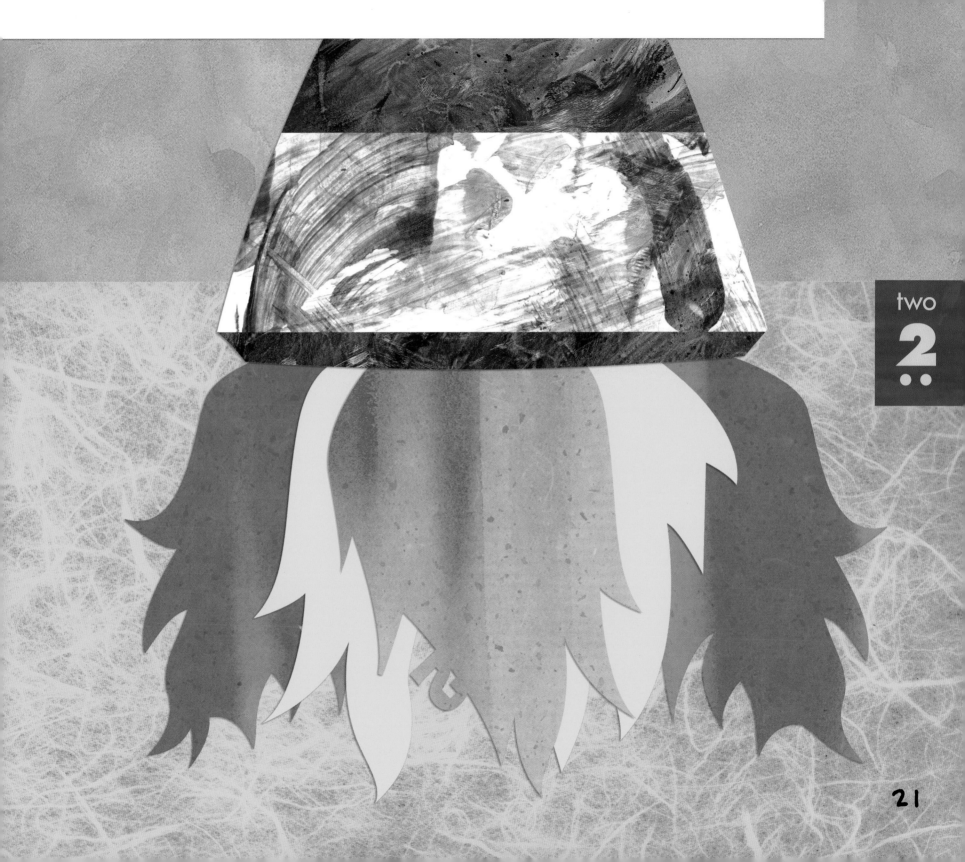

ONE shining rocket aims toward the stars. BLASTOFF!

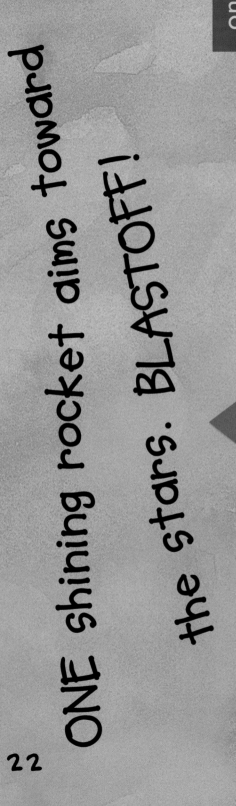

23

Fun Facts

- Yuri Gagarin of the Soviet Union was the first person to fly into space. His spaceship was called the Vostok.

- A rocket engine has about 3,000 times more power than a car engine of the same size.

- Radar helps those on the ground know where the rocket is after it flies into space.

- American astronaut Neil Armstrong was the first person to walk on the moon. Armstrong and Buzz Aldrin landed on the moon July 20, 1969.

- Astronauts use computers and look at the positions of stars to figure out where they are in space.

- The space shuttle was the first spacecraft that was able to be used more than once.

Look for all of the books in the Know Your Numbers series:

Ants At the Picnic: Counting by Tens
1-4048-1318-7

Bunches of Buttons: Counting by Tens
1-4048-1315-2

Downhill Fun:
A Counting Book About Winter
1-4048-0579-6

Eggs and Legs: Counting By Twos
1-4048-0945-7

Footprints in the Snow:
Counting By Twos
1-4048-0946-5

From the Garden:
A Counting Book About Growing Food
1-4048-0578-8

Hands Down: Counting By Fives
1-4048-0948-1

Lots of Ladybugs! Counting By Fives
1-4048-0944-9

On the Launch Pad:
A Counting Book About Rockets
1-4048-0581-8

One Big Building:
A Counting Book About Construction
1-4048-0580-X

One Checkered Flag:
A Counting Book About Racing
1-4048-0576-1

One Giant Splash:
A Counting Book About the Ocean
1-4048-0577-X

Pie for Piglets: Counting By Twos
1-4048-0943-0

Plenty of Petals: Counting by Tens
1-4048-1317-9

Speed, Speed, Centipede!
Counting by Tens
1-4048-1316-0

Starry Arms: Counting By Fives
1-4048-0947-3

Tail Feather Fun: Counting By Tens
1-4048-1319-5

Toasty Toes: Counting By Tens
1-4048-1320-9

Find the Numbers

Now you have finished reading the story, but a surprise still awaits you. Hidden in each picture is one of the numbers from 1 to 12. Can you find them all?

12 –near the top of the rocket

11 –near the center of the rocket

10 –near the center of the launch tower

9 –on the second spotlight from the left

8 –on the white fuel tank

7 –on the top right radar dish

6 –on the helmet of the astronaut on the top right of the elevator

5 –in the center of the third control panel from the left

4 –on the top of the upper right window

3 –connecting the truck to the launch tower

2 –toward the center of the right flame

1 –at the top of the rocket

On the Web

FactHound offers a safe, fun way to find Web sites related to this book. All of the sites on FactHound have been researched by our staff.

1. Visit *www.facthound.com*

2. Type in this special code: 1404805818

3. Click on the FETCH IT button.

Your trusty FactHound will fetch the best sites for you!